Kings and Queens

Written by A.N. George
Illustrated by David McAllister

MARKS &
SPENCER

Marks and Spencer p.l.c.
Baker Street, London W1U 8EP
www.marksandspencer.com

Copyright © Exclusive Editions 2001

This book was created by Monkey Puzzle Media Ltd

ISBN 1-84273-193-9

Printed in Dubai

Designer: Sarah Crouch
Cover design: Victoria Webb
Editor: Jon Richards
Artwork commissioning:
Roger Goddard-Coote
Project manager: Alex Edmonds

Contents

Druids worshipping at Stonehenge.

Who was Boudicca?

Around two thousand years ago, England was divided between various tribes who all had their own leaders, and these tribes were split into two races. In the north and the west, there were the remnants of a race called the Picts. Everywhere else were the Celts, fiery people who also lived in France and Spain. They were divided into various groups who often fought each other over land and possessions. One of these Celtic tribes was called the Iceni. Their home was in present-day East Anglia, and in AD 60 Boudicca was their queen.

PROBLEM CHIEFTAIN

The great British chieftain Caractacus was a major problem for the conquering Romans. He kept attacking their legions. In AD 50, the Romans defeated him, and Caractacus was taken to Rome and paraded in front of the jeering crowds. It is said that when he saw the magnificent buildings of Rome, he exclaimed: 'I wonder that the Romans, who possess such palaces, should envy the huts of the Britons.'

Did the Celts have a religion?

The early Britons believed in a religion called Druidism. It was based on respecting nature. The Druids believed that many places were sacred, including woods, forests, groves and springs. During one of their rituals, they would cut mistletoe from a sacred oak tree with a golden sickle. The Druids are believed to have conducted ceremonies at Stonehenge, the circle of enormous and ancient stones on Salisbury Plain in Wiltshire.

Why did Boudicca become famous?

When Boudicca's husband, King Prasutagus died in either AD 59 or 60, he left all his wealth to his two daughters and half his kingdom to his wife. The other half of the estate went to the Romans who had just conquered Britain. But this did not satisfy the Romans and they looted Boudicca's palace, took her land, and flogged the queen in front of her family and servants.

Did Boudicca fight the Romans?

Yes, she gathered a vast army of Britons and, probably in AD 61, went on the attack, determined to drive the Romans out of Britain. Soon, she had wiped out the settlements of Colchester, London and St Albans, all Roman strongholds. But the Romans fought back with an army of 10,000 men and Boudicca's army was defeated somewhere near where Warwickshire is today. Boudicca herself escaped but she later committed suicide by taking poison.

What was Britain like in AD 60?

What did Boudicca look like?
Early descriptions tell us that she was terrifying to look at. Very tall and strong, she had a mass of long hair that came down to her waist. According to the Roman writer Dio Cassius, it was bright red and often decorated with woad, a mixture of chalk and water. During battles, she used to ride a chariot drawn by horses. She had a very loud voice, which people could hear over the din of battle.

Did the Iceni take trophies when they attacked?
The Celts loved taking the heads of their enemies as trophies. They hung them up on temples, houses and gates. Numerous skulls have been found in the Walbrook, a river that used to run through London. They had probably been thrown there as offerings by Boudicca and her people when they sacked the city.

IN THE TIME OF THE CELTS, ENGLAND WAS FULL of marshes and huge, dark forests. In between the long lines of rolling hills, were large clearings where people cultivated food and built small villages. The Romans, however, started building roads and towns that later grew into many of the cities that we have today.

Where is Queen Boudicca buried?
Legend has it that Boudicca's followers buried her body in a secret place where the Romans could not find it. It is said that her grave lies under Platform 8 at King's Cross Station in London. Of course, no one knows for sure. The Iceni might have taken Boudicca's body back to their land in East Anglia.

The warrior-queen, Boudicca, drives her horses on to face the Roman's in battle.

BURNING THE CAKES

An ancient legend tells how King Alfred stumbled into a swineherd's cottage. The swineherd's wife, who did not recognize the king, said he could stay if he looked after the cakes she was baking while she went out. Some time later, the woman returned home to find Alfred dozing by the fire and the cakes burnt. She was about to tell him off when her husband turned up and recognized the king.

Was there a Roman king of Britain?

No. IN ROMAN TIMES, BRITAIN WAS JUST a province and it was ruled by the Roman emperor from Rome. But by the beginning of the fifth century AD, the Roman Empire was falling apart. Most of the Roman soldiers in Britain were needed to defend their country against the German tribes of central Europe. In 410, the last of the Romans left Britain, and by the end of the sixth century, the Roman occupation was a distant memory.

Who ruled Britain after the Romans left?

With the Romans gone, new invaders took over England. They were the Anglo-Saxons and they came from Germany. After landing on the East Anglian coast in 420, the Anglo-Saxons set up various kingdoms around the country, including Northumbria in the north, East Anglia in the east, Mercia in central England and Wessex, Essex, Sussex and Kent in the south. Each kingdom had its own Saxon ruler.

Did the Saxons get on well with each other?

No sooner had the Anglo-Saxon kings settled in Britain than they started fighting amongst themselves. Every so often, one kingdom would become bigger than the others and its king would call himself the king of the English. By 627, for example, King Edwin of Northumbria was so powerful that many recognized him as 'ruler of Britain'. Just five years later, in 632, the people of Mercia staged an attack on the Northumbrians. In 757, King Offa became ruler of all England. He treated the kingdoms outside Mercia as mere provinces.

Did the English live in peace under King Offa?

No. In 793, Viking ships were seen off the coast of England. It was the start of a sequence of raids that, by the middle of the ninth century, saw huge parts of Britain under Viking attack. Danes started settling in England until they had taken over the western part of the land and turned it into a kingdom called the Danelaw. From here they carried out raids on the neighbouring Saxon kingdoms. They kept on conquering until they came up against the only man in the country who could defeat them – Alfred the Great, king of Wessex.

How did Alfred beat the Vikings?

Alfred the Great

By 871, IT SEEMED THAT THE KINGDOM OF WESSEX WAS going to be conquered by Danes led by their merciless leader Guthorm. Alfred's father, Ethelwulf, and all of Alfred's brothers were dead. Still a young man, Alfred was forced to hide in a swamp in Athelney in Somerset. From there, he organized one raid after another until he conquered the Vikings at the Battle of Eddington in 878.

Did Alfred like being a warrior?
Alfred much preferred peace to war. He spent a lot of time praying and he rebuilt many churches that had been destroyed by the Vikings. He also spent a lot of time translating books. When no teachers could be found to teach children in England, he sent abroad for educated monks.

Who benefited from Alfred's reforms?
Alfred the Great spent the last twenty years of his life making England a safe place to live in. He built many new towns on the ruins of old Roman cities, and erected a large number of forts. Alfred also reorganized the army, which remained on duty even in harvest time when all able-bodied men were out in the fields.

Did Alfred banish the Vikings from England?
No, he had to make a treaty with Guthorm. The Vikings promised not to invade the kingdom of Wessex. In return, Alfred had to accept that Guthorm was the rightful ruler of the Danelaw. For a while, both parties lived in an uneasy alliance. But the Vikings would not give up their dreams of ruling the whole of England.

Viking ships approach the coast of England.

Did the Vikings ever conquer the whole of England?

AFTER ALFRED THE GREAT DIED IN 899, HIS SUCCESSORS TRIED to win parts of England back from the Vikings. But all their efforts were in vain. In 978, Vikings from Denmark started attacking England again. Now there was no great king like Alfred to hold them at bay. By 1016, a Danish king called Cnut was sitting on the English throne. He ruled over England, Denmark and Norway at the same time.

Was King Cnut really called that?

Yes, but English historians changed the name to Canute to make it sound more English. People did not like the idea that Canute was a Viking, and it was easier for them to think of him as English if he had a name they could pronounce.

Did becoming a king change Cnut?

In his youth King Cnut was known for his ferocious courage. His father, the Danish king Svein Forkbeard, had taught his son all about Viking pillaging and looting. But when he became king of England, Cnut learnt very quickly to listen to the earls and advisors at court as they were older and wiser than him. He brought security and justice to England, and was said to have become more English than the English!

Was Cnut a good king?

Cnut put his pillaging background behind him to become a good king. He worked hard to spread learning through his kingdom, and England became prosperous under his rule. Cnut also became a devout Christian and made a long pilgrimage to Rome to meet the Pope and ask forgiveness for killing people during his battles.

Did Cnut really stop the sea?

Legend has it that King Cnut's subjects kept showering him with praise and telling him how powerful he was. Some even insisted that the sea would obey his every command. The king promptly had his throne carried to the seashore. There he ordered the tide to withdraw. Needless to say, the sea did not obey and King Cnut was drenched. The wise ruler had made his point. No man was as powerful as God or nature.

King Cnut commands the sea to withdraw.

Lady Godiva prepares to ride around the city of Coventry.

Were the Vikings scared of anything?

Very few people have been able to match

the Vikings' fierceness. When attacking a coastal settlement, they killed everyone they met, including babies and children. But even the bravest Viking warrior was afraid of ghosts. The merest hint of a white shape glowing in the dark would petrify a Viking. He would think that his dead ancestors had come to fetch him to the land of the dead.

LADY GODIVA

One of Cnut's earls, a Dane called Leofric, imposed heavy taxes on the people of Coventry. His Saxon wife, Lady Godiva, objected and made him a very special bet. She promised to ride around Coventry naked. If the people stayed in behind closed doors and did not peep at her, Leofric must reduce the taxes. But if just one person took a peek, the taxes stayed. Next day, Lady Godiva rode around naked. Nobody peeked, and the taxes were reduced.

Why was Harold known as Harefoot?

In 1037, Cnut was succeeded as king of England by his son Harold. He was known as Harefoot, because he could run as fast as a hare. His running was better than his ruling though, and he was a much poorer king than his father.

Who dug up his brother's body?

Cnut had another son, named Hardicnut, who was furious when Harefoot inherited the throne. So he invaded England in 1040, only to find that his brother had already died! Hardicnut took his revenge anyway, by digging up his brother's body and throwing it into a marsh.

Who died at a wedding?

Hardicnut was an unpopular king and the English were delighted that his reign lasted only two years. He died after having a fit while proposing the toast at a wedding.

Was England peaceful when Harold was king?

Harold had not been king for long when a Viking king called Hardrada invaded the north of England. With him was Harold's own brother Tostig, who had been exiled from England. Harold and his army marched north and on September 25, 1066 drove Hardrada and Tostig's forces away from the shores of England.

How did Harold celebrate his victory over the Vikings?

Just as Harold and his men started celebrating their victory over Hardrada and Tostig, they received devastating news. William of Normandy and his men were sailing to England, determined to snatch the crown from Harold. Their ships had already left France and the wind was in their favour. They would reach the shores of England in a few days.

King Harold

ROYAL HUMOUR

When King Hardrada once joked that Harold II would soon be forced to hand over a big part of England, Harold replied, 'I'll only give you six feet.' Then he looked the Viking up and down and added, 'No, seven, seeing as you're taller than most men.' Not long afterwards, Hardrada was killed in battle. His grave was about seven feet long.

Why did Halley's Comet appear in 1066?

HAROLD GODWINSSON WAS THE SON OF GODWIN, the powerful Earl of Wessex, who had been advisor to King Edward the Confessor. When Edward died in 1066, Harold was crowned as the new king of England. William of Normandy was furious. He had grown up with Edward, and had received a promise from him that he would be the next king. William had also been made a promise by Harold. When he was shipwrecked in France, Harold had sworn to support William's claim to the English crown. When Halley's Comet rocketed across the sky in 1066, people believed it was a sign that God was angry at the breaking of these two promises.

What did Harold do when he heard that the Normans were about to invade England?

He turned his army round and started marching south right away. He reached London on October 5, and let his men have a well earned rest. Locals provided the army with food while Harold gathered reinforcements. But he knew that his men were too weary to fight another battle.

What kind of weapons did Harold's army use?

Harold's army was made up mostly of foot-soldiers. They used heavy axes which they had to wield with both hands. As long as they stayed high up on a hill, there was not much the Normans or any other enemy could do to defeat them.

Where did Harold's forces meet William the Conqueror's army?

The two forces clashed near Hastings on October 14. The English fought bravely but they were tired after the battle with Hardrada. The Normans managed to coax them down from the hills, where they were massacred. Harold was wounded and quickly died. Some say he was shot in the eye by an archer; others that he was dragged down from his horse and lanced. William of Normandy was the new king.

King Harold is injured as an arrow hits him directly in the eye.

When did William of Normandy reach England?

WILLIAM'S FORCES LANDED AT PEVENSEY ON September 28, 1066. They were well prepared to fight the English. They rode on horseback and their favourite weapon was the lance. Some of the soldiers also used maces, which were heavy clubs with an iron head. Others in the army were skilled with the sword or longbow.

How do we know what happened at the Battle of Hastings?

The Battle of Hastings is shown in a famous work of art called the Bayeux Tapestry. Embroidered on bleached linen, it shows not only the battle but the preparations for it. It also shows the English retreating in defeat from Hastings, and Harold being killed. The last part is missing. Perhaps it was never completed. Experts think the tapestry was made in Winchester, England, for Odo, the bishop of Bayeux. He was William of Normandy's half-brother and helped plan the invasion of England.

When did William become the king of England?

AFTER WINNING THE BATTLE OF HASTINGS, WILLIAM MADE his way to London. On the way there, his men looted and pillaged farms and estates. On Christmas Day 1066, William was crowned king of England. The ceremony took place in the newly built Westminster Abbey. He became known as William the Conqueror.

Did William the Conqueror speak English?

He spoke French, as did his followers the Normans. They believed that French culture was the most advanced in Europe, looked down on the English language and were disgusted at the thought of having to speak in such a coarse tongue.

Did William the Conqueror's coronation go smoothly?

At one point during the coronation ceremony, the French noblemen heard shouting outside the abbey and thought that their new subjects were rebelling. In fact, the Archbishop of York was trying to get the English crowds to cheer. The French, fearing the worst, set fire to the buildings around the abbey and William was crowned to the acrid smell of burning.

How did William treat his Saxon enemies?

Immediately after the coronation, many Saxon earls and barons were stripped of their property and removed from positions of power. The land was taken from them and given to French noblemen. Anyone who showed hostility to the Normans lost all their belongings and their houses were burnt down. Even so, there were still many uprisings. In 1067, the people of Wales and Kent tried to rebel against the new king. Then, in 1070 and 1071, there were rebellions in the Midlands. But William the Conqueror crushed all opposition and by 1072 was the undisputed ruler of all England.

The king directs operations as yet another Norman castle is built.

PROTECTING THE HUNT

William the Conqueror loved hunting in his royal forests. No one else but him and the members of his court were allowed to hunt there. People who were caught stealing deer or other animals from the king's forests were fined or thrown into prison. Sometimes they had a hand chopped off or an eye gouged out. These measures did not scare everyone off. Some English people saw it as their duty to steal from a foreign king.

What is the Domesday Book?

WILLIAM WANTED TO KNOW EXACTLY WHAT EVERYONE IN ENGLAND possessed so he could tax them. In December 1085, he decided to carry out a survey. Officials were sent all around the country to make records. All the details were put down in a book divided into two volumes. The English, unhappy about the fact that they were going to be charged more tax, dubbed it the Domesday Book. It still exists today, kept safe in the Public Record Office in London. It shows that the king owned 20 per cent of all the land in England. Another 25 per cent was owned by the Church, whilst an impressive 50 per cent was controlled by Norman barons. Only 5 per cent was in the hands of the Anglo-Saxons.

Did William change the way England was run?

The new king did not trust the English. He stripped the Church of its power and made his French friend Lan Franc the Archbishop of Canterbury. He claimed all the land in the country as his own. Then he leased it out to barons he trusted. The barons, or vassals as they were called, hired the land out to lords of the manors. And the lords hired parts of that land out to the poorer folk. The new king also built lots of castles, so that all this hiring out could be ruled over with an iron fist.

Did William build castles in London?

The Tower of London and Windsor Castle are perhaps the best known castles built by William the Conqueror. The part of the Tower of London built by him is known as the White Tower. Over the years, other kings added to the building.

How did the lords make money?

Corn was grown all over England and people had to take it to the mill where it was ground into flour. The mill belonged to the lord on whose land they lived and he charged them a share of the corn for using it. Sometimes the lord of the manor also owned the village oven and people had to pay him for using that too.

When did William die?

William spent the last years of his life fighting his enemies in Normandy. In 1086, he visited England for the last time. A year later, during a battle, his horse stumbled outside Rouen. The king was thrown to the ground, and six weeks later, on September 7, 1087, he died.

The two volumes of the Domesday Book.

ROBIN OF SHERWOOD

While Richard was away crusading, people in England suffered hardship. No one, it seemed, had any money left for food after taxes had been collected. A few brave souls took to the forests, poaching from the king's lands and stealing from the rich as they passed from one baron's estate to another. The exploits of these unknown men gave rise to the legend of Robin Hood and the outlaws of Sherwood Forest.

Who was Richard the Lionheart's mother?

She was a lady called Eleanor of Aquitaine, and Richard was her favourite son. She taught him music and poetry, and encouraged him to learn as many languages as possible. Richard learnt a good number, but he never spoke English at all. When he grew up and the Christian princes were preparing for the Crusades, Eleanor was often overheard boasting how her Richard was the 'great one and the good'.

The legendary outlaw, Robin Hood.

Who threatened to sell the city of London?

Even before he became king, Richard had decided to go off and fight in the Third Crusade. He raised money through taxes and by selling off some of the Crown's assets. At one point he even threatened to sell the city of London if he could get a good price for it. In December 1189, the same year he was crowned, he set off on the Crusades with Philip II of France and Frederick I of Germany.

What were the Crusades?

They were a series of holy wars fought between Muslims and Christians who both wanted to control the area that was known as Palestine, where Jesus had lived and died. Christians did not like the idea of these holy places of pilgrimage being in the hands of Muslims. The Muslims, however, claimed that they had always lived there.

Who was Richard the Lionheart?

HE WAS A DISTANT RELATIVE OF WILLIAM THE CONQUEROR.

His father, Henry II, was French, but Richard was born at Beaumont Palace near Oxford in England. As an adult, he was famous for his bravery, which earned him the nickname 'Coeur de Lion' or Lionheart. His dedication to the Christian faith and his love of poetry were unrivalled by any other king of the time. Not that he spent a great deal of time composing verses in Britain. During his ten-year reign, which began in 1189 after the death of his father, he only spent a total of six months on British soil.

Was Richard's campaign in the Holy Land successful?

Richard and Philip II of France managed to win the city of Acre, near Jerusalem, from the Muslims. But then the two kings quarrelled and Philip returned home, leaving Richard on his own. The king of England fought on but could not take Jerusalem from the Muslim ruler Saladin. Richard did manage, however, to negotiate a deal that allowed Christian pilgrims to visit the holy city without fear of persecution.

Who was Saladin?

He was a fierce and very intelligent warrior. As fiercely Muslim as Richard the Lionheart was Christian, he built mosques and universities and encouraged writers to write about Islam and the holy wars against Christian kings like Richard. Under his rule, the Muslim countries of the eastern Mediterranean flourished.

What happened to Richard on the way home?

O N HIS WAY HOME FROM THE CRUSADES, RICHARD'S SHIP WAS CAUGHT in a storm and wrecked in the Adriatic Sea. Richard donned a disguise and tried to travel home through the lands of his enemies in Austria, but was captured. His mother, Queen Eleanor, had to raise a hefty ransom for the king's release. The money was collected from the people, and in early 1194 Richard was released and returned home.

How did Richard the Lionheart die?

Soon after he had returned from the Crusades, Richard was off on his travels again. He sailed to France to collect money from the good people of Chalus, who had found treasure on his land. While laying siege to a castle, Richard was struck in the shoulder by an arrow. The wound refused to heal, and in April 1199 he died. Richard was buried in Fontevrault, and the lion-hearted king's heart was given as a gift to the cathedral of Rouen.

Who was John the Bad?

JOHN WAS RICHARD THE LIONHEART'S YOUNGEST BROTHER.

He was the only one of Henry II's sons who had been left with no land to rule after his father's death, which led to people calling him John Lackland. While Richard was missing in Austria on his way home from the Crusades, John plotted to prevent the king ever returning home. He wanted the throne for himself. During this time, he encouraged the barons of the country to disobey Richard.

King John commands his soldiers to rescue his ill-gotten treasure from the river.

How much did John the Bad like treasure?

John was famous for his love of magnificent clothes, sumptuous feasts, and especially treasure. By the end of his reign he was fighting with his own barons, and a well known story tells how the king tried to carry the treasures he had stolen from them across a river. The tide came in and all the treasures were washed away, leaving King John heartbroken. He died shortly afterwards.

16

Did Richard the Lionheart forgive his brother when he returned from the Crusades?

When Richard the Lionheart returned from the Crusades, he forgave John for trying to steal his throne. He genuinely believed that his younger brother had been led astray by the crafty barons and the people at court. When Richard died, John inherited the throne at last, and became the king of England.

Why was John called the Bad?

WHILE JOHN WAS ON THE THRONE, THE FRENCH MANAGED
to win back their land in Normandy, Maine and Anjou from the English. John was forced into war to try to win them back. To pay for his armies, he had to tax his people. When the battles went badly for him, the king returned to England defeated and poor. He then had to command his people to pay even heavier taxes. This did nothing to improve his popularity. People thought that, compared to his brother Richard, he was not much of a king.

Did the Pope think King John was bad?

King John even incurred the anger of the Pope, by refusing the Pope's nomination of a cardinal named Stephen Langton as the next Archbishop of Canterbury. When John offered the office to one of his own favourites instead, the Pope shut down all the churches in England. John reacted by stealing some of the Church's treasures. The Pope then had him excommunicated – in other words, thrown out of the Church.

Did anyone try to rebel against King John?

Most ordinary people had no choice but to pay the heavy taxes demanded by the king. But the barons had the power to fight back. In 1215, they rebelled against their king. At the end of the uprising, in a meadow at Runnymede on the south bank of the Thames, John was forced to sign a document called the Magna Carta.

The Magna Carta

What was the Magna Carta?

It was a special document that guaranteed people certain rights to protect them from greedy kings. Barons could not be taxed without their consent. People were protected from corrupt officials who were always trying to demand more tax. Freemen could not be arrested, tried and imprisoned by anyone except a jury. At the time, the Magna Carta did not mean much to ordinary people, but it became the basis of many rights that we all enjoy today.

Who dug up the body of bad King John?

King John died in 1216, still as unpopular as when he had inherited the throne of England from his brother Richard. His nine-year-old son, Henry III, inherited the throne. Henry never forgot his father. When he grew up, he decided that Westminster Abbey was not grand enough for grand kings like him. So he had it rebuilt. Then he dug up the body of John the Bad and had it reburied in a magnificent new grave.

WANDERING MINSTREL

Popular legend has it that a wandering minstrel called Blondel went off in search of Richard the Lionheart when he was held captive in Austria. One day, the minstrel heard a familiar song drifting out of a tower window. Could it be the king? Blondel started singing the words and the prisoner in the tower answered. Blondel informed the local monks, who quickly sent word to England. Soon the English were raising money for the king's ransom.

What were the Wars of the Roses?

BEGINNING IN 1455, THE ENGLISH FAMILIES KNOWN AS

the houses of York and Lancaster fought for the English crown. Their battles were called the Wars of the Roses, because the Yorkists' symbol was a white rose and the Lancastrians' a red one. By 1471, it seemed the house of York had a firm grip on the throne with the reign of Edward IV. The white rose appeared to have won. But the wars continued when, in April 1483, Edward died unexpectedly.

Who were the Woodvilles?
The older prince was named King Edward V, but because he was so young his uncle Richard was appointed his guardian or 'protector'. When the Woodville family, the relatives of Edward's mother Elizabeth Woodville, tried to gain influence with the young king, Richard took drastic action. He locked the two princes away in the Tower of London before Edward could be crowned. Then he took the throne himself, and was crowned as Richard III.

Did Edward IV have any heirs?
He had two sons, Edward and Richard, but they were still young when he died. Edward, the rightful heir to the throne, was thirteen and Richard was eleven.

Who was Richard III?
Richard III was the brother of Edward IV, and the uncle of the heirs to the throne, Edward and Richard. When the young princes disappeared, people were convinced that Richard had killed them. This has never been proved, but it has led to Richard being portrayed as one of the most evil of kings. Some historians wrote that he was destined to be evil when he was born with a full set of teeth!

Richard III is run-through at the Battle of Bosworth.

Was Richard III a good or a bad king?

BEFORE HE WAS CROWNED, RICHARD WAS KNOWN

as a just man who would not accept bribes. While governing some parts of England for his brother, Edward IV, he was known to help out the poor and the needy. He even got permission from his brother to hold fairs so that people could trade with their neighbours. As a king, he did more for the common people than any other ruler before him. He stopped all taxes on books and he made sure that all laws were written in English instead of Latin so that everyone could understand them. Richard also started a postal service and gave grants to poor students

Richard III watches the two young princes sleeping in their quarters.

Was Richard III really a hunchback?

The politician Sir Thomas More and the famous playwright William Shakespeare both describe Richard as 'crookback' or 'crouchback', but they were writing a long time after his death. He is portrayed as a hunchback in Shakespearean plays, but this may just make it easier for audiences to identify him as a villain. He was certainly a very capable fighter, and was also known to be a very elegant dancer.

What were Richard III's last words?

At the Battle of Bosworth Field in August 1485, Richard found himself completely surrounded by the soldiers of Henry Tudor. Henry was descended from the house of Lancaster and wanted to win the throne back for the family of the red rose. A number of lords who Richard thought he could trust had betrayed him and joined Henry's army. Richard fought with incredible bravery, but when he was cut down the Wars of the Roses were over. His last words were: 'Treason! Treason! Treason!'

DEATH OF THE PRINCES

To this day, no one knows for certain if King Richard III was responsible for the deaths of the young princes Edward and Richard. In 1674, two skeletons were found in the Tower. Were they the bones of the missing boys? In the 1930s, the skeletons were examined by experts. They could not decide how old the bones were or whether they belonged to boys or girls. The mystery remained unsolved.

Where was Richard III buried?

After his death on the battlefield Richard III was not laid to rest in Westminster Abbey like many other kings. Instead, he was buried in a remote church. Some years later, vandals broke into his grave and stole the body. No one knows what happened to it.

Henry VIII practises his falconry techniques.

Did the young Prince Henry go to school?

Like many rich people of his time, Henry had his own personal tutor. He was a priest called John Skelton. Henry's lessons included English, French, Latin, Arithmetic and Divinity. Henry was also very good at chess, an early form of tennis, bowls and martial arts. He also liked composing songs. As he grew older, Henry became rather fond of gambling, a pastime that he would enjoy for the rest of his life. He also jousted on horseback, and hunted with falcons. A lot of women were attracted to Henry, and it was no wonder. He was tall, handsome and sporty, and was heir to the throne of England.

What sports did ordinary people play?

When Henry became king, he forbade ordinary people to play sports such as football or games with cards or dice. He wanted everyone to concentrate on their work. In those days, people had to work 17 hours a day or more! The only sport that was allowed was archery, because Henry thought it might come in useful if people ever had to defend their country.

Who was Henry VIII?

HENRY VIII WAS THE SON OF HENRY TUDOR WHO HAD defeated Richard III at the Battle of Bosworth Field. He was born on June 28, 1491. As he was the king's second son he did not expect to inherit the throne of England. But his elder brother Arthur died young. Henry was crowned in 1509 when he was just 18 years old.

How much did Henry VIII enjoy his food?

Henry loved food with a passion, and ate huge meals. During a dinner held in honour of a French king, he and his guests ate 5,000 chickens and drank 25,000 litres of beer! At another meal, laid on by the Marquis of Exeter, Henry sampled stewed sparrows, pheasant, stork, heron, venison, roast chicken, gulls, rabbit and blanchmange. All this feasting was, of course, not very good for the king's health. In later life he became obese and suffered from many diseases. He could no longer fit into his armour. Indeed, during the last five years of his reign, he could no longer stand up.

LITTLE JACK HORNER

It is said that an abbot once sent Henry VIII twelve documents hidden in a pie. The documents made Henry the owner of twelve manors. But the messenger who carried the pie managed to sneak one document out from under the crust. It made him the owner of a house called the Manor of Mells in Somerset. The messenger's name was Little Jack Horner and he became famous when a nursery rhyme was written about how he found himself a 'plum' home.

How many times did Henry VIII marry?

He was married six times. His first wife was

Catherine of Aragon, his brother's widow, who bore him a daughter, Mary. Henry separated from Catherine and married her maid of honour, Anne Boleyn, who also produced a daughter, Elizabeth. Desperate for a son, Henry had her beheaded for infidelity. Next came Jane Seymour who, in October 1537, gave birth to a boy, Edward. She died soon after, and Henry married Anne of Cleves. He divorced her for Catherine Howard. She followed poor Anne Boleyn to the block, before Henry finally married Catherine Parr.

HENRY'S SPECIAL FRIEND

Henry VIII had all manner of advisors at court to run his affairs and to keep him amused. One special servant had the rather daunting task of talking to the king when he was on the toilet. Popular topics would have included hunting, jousting, war and women. It was probably best not to talk about marriage!

King Henry VIII lived in Hampton Court palace for many years.

Why did Henry argue with the Pope?

Henry wanted to make sure he had a son who would inherit the throne. When Henry's first wife, Catherine of Aragon failed to give birth to a healthy boy, he decided to divorce her and marry someone else. But the Pope refused to give Henry a divorce. So Henry declared himself head of the Christian Church in England and at the same time declared himself free of his wife.

What did Henry think of Anne of Cleves' portrait painter?

Not a lot. Anne had been recommended as a wife by Henry's advisor Thomas Cromwell. Henry had never laid eyes on her before the wedding, he had merely seen a portrait of her. When he did finally see her, she was not at all to his liking. The two soon got divorced and Henry married Catherine Howard. But he was soon convinced she was being unfaithful, so she was beheaded. Henry's last wife was a widow, Catherine Parr. She achieved the difficult feat of surviving Henry, who died on January 28, 1547.

21

Who were Queen Elizabeth I's parents?

Elizabeth I was the daughter of King Henry VIII

by his second wife, Anne Boleyn. She was born on September 7, 1533. As a child, she was only third in line to the throne. Her half-brother, Edward, the son of Jane Seymour, was king after Henry VIII but died at the age of 15. He was succeeded by Mary, the daughter of Catherine of Aragon, but in 1558 she also died. So Elizabeth became queen of England and was crowned on January 15, 1559.

How many times did Elizabeth marry?

Elizabeth was afraid that if she married, her husband would try to influence her decisions. Some of her favourite men at court included the dashing Robert Dudley, Christopher Hatton who was famous for his dancing, and Walter Raleigh, a soldier and explorer. Another close friend of the queen was Francis Drake, who she gave a magnificent sword with the words 'To my dear pyrate' carved on the handle. But despite having all these favourites, Elizabeth I never married.

Was Queen Elizabeth popular with her subjects?

Elizabeth was very popular. Everywhere she went, huge crowds gathered to cheer her. People thought up all sorts of magnificent names to call her, such as Gloriana, to show how glorious she was, and Virgin Queen, to show that she had dedicated her life to her people and not to a husband. The poet Edmund Spenser even wrote a poem about her called *The Faerie Queen*.

Was Elizabeth a happy child?

Elizabeth I had a very difficult childhood, which left her shy and insecure about her looks even as an adult. As a little girl, she was always being moved from one palace to another. Her father Henry VIII, who had wanted a boy, ignored her. Luckily, the young princess had a dedicated tutor called Kate Ashley. She encouraged her to learn Latin, Greek, French and Italian. But, even though she was respected for her intelligence, Elizabeth still hated her looks. When she grew up, she had all portraits of herself destroyed.

English ships attack the Spanish Armada off the coast of England.

Queen Elizabeth studies her reflection in a mirror.

What kind of bed did wealthy Elizabethans like?
During Elizabeth I's reign people started to stuff their mattresses with feathers rather than straw. Four-poster beds were very popular, and people liked them so much that they left them to their descendants in their wills.

Did Elizabeth I ever visit her friends?

In a bid to stay in touch with the people of her land, Queen Elizabeth I went on what she called 'progresses'. During these she would stay with rich families while she toured the local area. These visits usually cost the hosts a great deal, often sending them into near-bankruptcy. Elizabeth would bring her whole court, servants and advisors with her. She even brought her own four-poster bed.

Did England prosper under Elizabeth?
When Elizabeth came to the throne in 1559, England was considered a poor country. Even the nobility were starved of cash. The new queen was to change all that. Under her, England was to become one of the most powerful and respected nations in the world. There was trading on a global scale. The wool and weaving trades flourished and other countries were colonized. Queen Elizabeth loved music, poetry and drama, so those became popular too. Geniuses like the playwrights Ben Jonson and William Shakespeare lived during her reign.

How did people cook in Elizabethan times?
Most people cooked their food over an open fire. Meat was roasted on a spit. Often, it was the job of the family dog to turn the spit. It would run round and round on a treadmill. People also baked food by putting it inside an iron box and then burying the box in the hot ashes of the fire.

What were houses like during Elizabethan times?
Up until Elizabethan times, houses were designed to keep people out so they looked more like castles than houses. In a time of prosperity, Elizabeth's subjects were not bothered about people attacking them, so they built houses with large windows that would let in a lot of light and also show off their furniture. They used wood rather than stones for building and had beautiful gardens, designed as places of rest and relaxation.

THE ARMADA

In 1588 King Philip II of Spain decided to conquer England and sent a fleet of 130 warships to invade. Elizabeth I fought back with 197 ships under the leadership of Howard of Effingham and Sir Francis Drake. While the Spanish Armada was moored in Calais, the English set fire to some of their own ships and sent them into the harbour to cause chaos. Many of the Spanish ships managed to escape the flames, but were caught in a storm and sunk. The invasion had failed.

Which queen was always ill?

THE DAUGHTER OF JAMES II, QUEEN ANNE WAS BORN

on February 6, 1665. She was the last ruler of England from a family called the Stuarts. Anne reigned from 1702 to 1714. According to historians of the time she was very beautiful but a succession of illnesses left their mark on her. At the age of 12, she contracted smallpox, which left her with scars on her face. She also suffered from gout, an illness caused by eating too much rich food. As she grew older, Anne developed rheumatism. She also grew so fat that she had to be hoisted on to her throne.

Queen Anne was also terribly short-sighted, and had to screw up her eyes to see properly. This made many people who saw her think she was frowning all the time.

Who was Queen Anne's husband?

Queen Anne was married to Prince George of Denmark. He was said to be rather a dull fellow who spent most of his time trying to solve mathematical puzzles.

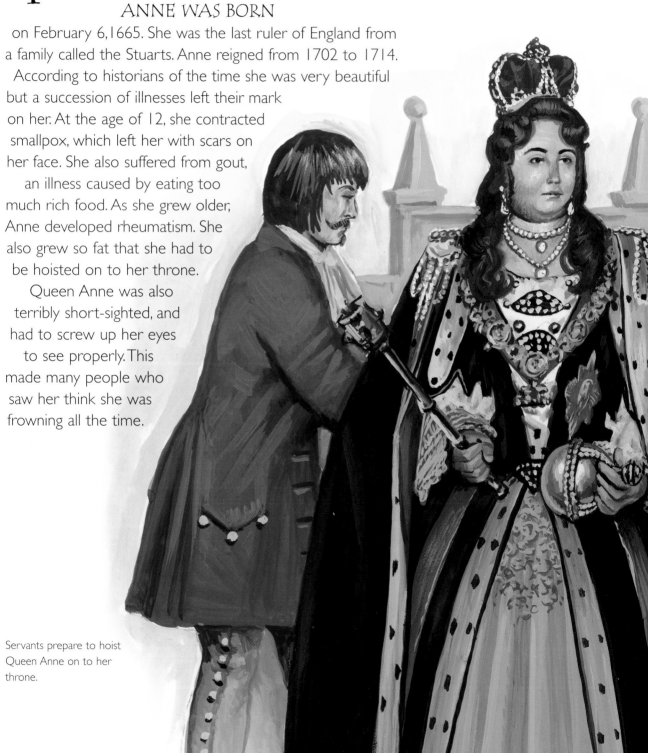

Servants prepare to hoist Queen Anne on to her throne.

QUEEN ANNE'S REVENGE

Blackbeard was one of the most infamous pirates that ever lived. During Queen Anne's War he was a privateer, raiding for the queen. Then he turned to real piracy, keeping any treasure he looted just for himself. In 1717, he captured a French slave ship which he equipped with 40 cannons. He named his new pirate ship, *Queen Anne's Revenge*, in honour of his favourite queen who had died three years earlier. When Blackbeard was finally captured he lost his beloved ship and his head. But the wreck of *Queen Anne's Revenge* has recently been found off the coast of North Carolina, USA.

Was Queen Anne a successful ruler?

Yes, SHE WAS THE MOST POPULAR MONARCH

since Elizabeth I. During her reign, more countries were added to the expanding British Empire. The Greenwich Royal Park in London was opened to public acclaim. The astronomer Edmund Halley discovered the famous comet that was named after him. English ships were plying their trade all around the world and Queen Anne's armies won many battles. It was a time of prosperity.

What were privateers?

Privateers were really pirate ships in disguise. Their owners and sailors would obtain a 'letter of marque' from their king or queen, giving them permission to attack and loot enemy ships. The sailors would then keep most of the treasure and pay a portion to their rulers. It was an economical way for kings and queens to increase their wealth as well as their power on the high seas. Queen Anne was very fond of using privateers.

What was Queen Anne's War?

Queen Anne's War was fought between England and France and started just before Anne came to power. The two European nations were fighting over which one of them should have control of large areas of land in Canada and America. At the end of the war, which lasted until 1713, Newfoundland and Nova Scotia became British territories. It was a big success for Queen Anne.

Who hunted from a chariot?

Like many other noblewomen of her time, Queen Anne took great delight in playing card games. She also enjoyed strolling around her gardens with friends. Her favourite beverage was tea, often drunk with a nip of gin in it to ease the pain of her various ailments. On occasion, the Queen also enjoyed hunting. But because of her rheumatism, she had to use a horse-drawn chariot instead of riding on a horse.

What is Queen Anne furniture?

It is a style of furniture that was popular during the reign of Queen Anne. Chairs, beds and desks had curved legs called 'cabriole' legs. Carpenters often made this kind of furniture using walnut, maple or cherry wood.

Did Queen Anne have any children?

Yes, she had seventeen children! But only one survived infancy. His name was William, Duke of Gloucester, and many people said he was destined for greatness. Unfortunately, he was no healthier than his mother, and died soon after his twelfth birthday. When Queen Anne herself died on August 1, 1714, the English throne passed to her German cousin, who became George I.

'Mad' King George

When did George III become king?

G EORGE III BECAME KING IN 1760.
HE WAS OF GERMAN
blood but had spent all of his childhood in England. George was in fact very proud to be British. By the time he came to power, England had a government led by a prime minister. The king often did not see eye to eye with the prime minister and other politicians and schemed to take power away from them.

BETTER CONDITIONS

While George III was arguing with his politicians, the ordinary people were working to better their lot. A law was passed allowing people to strike if they were unhappy with their wages or their working conditions. Catholics were allowed to vote in elections for the first time, and the slave trade in England was finally abolished.

What kind of childhood did George III have?

George III is believed to have had a miserable childhood. Despised by both parents for being a weakling, he was often scolded by his mother and ignored by his father. He was prone to crying in front of guests, a habit which infuriated both his parents. As an adult, he also stuttered. King George quarrelled with his own servants, hated the trappings of royalty and preferred the simple things of life. This led people at court to call him Farmer George.

Did George III have a family of his own?

George married Charlotte Sophia in 1761. The couple were devoted to each other and had fifteen children, nine sons and six daughters. Family life was very important to George. He lavished a lot of time on his children and often took them on holiday to English seaside resorts.

500　　　　　　1000　　　　　　1500　　1760–1820　2000

Did George III really go mad?

UNFORTUNATELY, KING GEORGE STARTED GOING MAD SOME time in the 1780s. People thought the stress of his country's many battles had been too much for him. Today, we know he suffered from a rare blood disease called porphyria.

What was the Boston Tea Party?
When George III was crowned king, America was still an English colony. But running America from across the Atlantic Ocean proved to be expensive. In 1767, the English parliament decided to tax the Americans, with the extra income to the government going to help police the colonies. The new law did not go down well in America. On December 16, 1773, some men in Boston refused to pay tax on a shipment of tea and threw it in the water. The incident was nicknamed the Boston Tea Party. A war erupted between England and her colonists in America. By July 4, 1776, the Americans had declared independence from Britain. George III was blamed for the loss of a valuable colony.

Did England and America make peace after the Tea Party?
British naval officers had the habit of kidnapping American sailors. They forced them to abandon their ships and serve in the English navy instead. This did not go down too well with the American government. Another war broke out between the two nations until the English promised not to hijack any more American sailors.

Did King George III carry on as king when he was mad?
He tried, but his son George, Prince of Wales, had to be made Regent in 1811. This meant he ruled in the king's place. The Prince Regent had a reputation as a lady's man. In 1785, he had secretly married a Catholic woman called Maria Fitzherbert. The British government did not accept the marriage and in 1795, the Prince Regent was married again, this time to Caroline of Brunswick. When George III died in 1820, the Prince Regent became king in his place. He was crowned George IV, but poor Caroline was not allowed to attend the coronation.

Settlers, dressed as Native Americans, empty crates of tea into the sea at Boston.

Was George IV a popular king?
The period when George IV ruled is known as the Regency period. It was not a happy time for many ordinary people. Twenty years of war with Napoleon had left many people penniless and out of work. There were food shortages and the prices of many things were beyond most workers' means. Despite all this, George IV lived in lavish splendour. He built a magnificent palace in Brighton where he used to spy on guests when they came for dinner.

What was George IV's favourite food?
The Prince Regent loved his food. His favourite foods for tea included regalia of cucumbers; calves' head pie; boiled rabbit; pigeon stew; whole pig slit down the back and boiled with herbs; stew of silver eel; buttered lobsters and bombarded veal. For dessert, he enjoyed calves' foot pudding with sliced almonds and lemon juice.

Queen Victoria and her beloved Prince Albert.

When did Victoria become queen of the UK?

O N JUNE 24, 1837, PRINCESS VICTORIA WAS WOKEN UP EARLY.

Her uncle had died and she had become the new queen of the UK. She was only 18 but she took her responsibilities seriously. At first she relied heavily on Lord Melbourne, the prime minister and leader of the ruling Whig party, for advice. But as she gained more confidence, she started to trust her own judgement in her work.

HARD WORK

In 1840, only 20 per cent of children went to school. The others had to work. The lucky ones were made apprentices and learnt a trade, while others became servants. Some poor children started working in coal-mines at the age of five and it was known for them to work 16 hours a day. During the Victorian age this was eventually cut down to ten hours for both children and adults.

When was Victoria born?

Queen Victoria was born on May 24, 1819. Her grandfather was King George III and her father was Prince Edward, Duke of Kent. Queen Victoria's mother was a beautiful German woman called Victoria of Saxe-Coburg. The young princess was christened Alexandrina Victoria. Her mother called her Victoria, but everyone else called her by her pet name, Drina.

Did Victoria have a happy childhood?

Queen Victoria had a very sheltered childhood. Her mother was scared that one of her relatives might try to assassinate her to stop her becoming ruler of the UK when her uncle, King William IV, died. So the princess was always watched over by guards, even during her lessons and especially when having meals. When she went up or down the stairs, someone always used to hold her hand, in case she was knocked over. Despite all this, Princess Drina was a very happy and cheerful child.

Who did Victoria marry?

She married a German cousin of hers, called Prince Albert of Saxe-Coburg. In 1839, Albert visited Queen Victoria in England. She was very taken with him, but Albert was not so sure about his feelings or the idea of being married to the queen of the UK. However, Victoria won him over and in time the pair became inseparable. They had nine children.

Was Prince Albert popular with the British?

Some mistrusted Albert because he spoke English with a thick German accent. But Prince Albert worked very hard for the British people. He forced Victoria to think about social problems, and helped bring about a law to improve children's working conditions in factories. He also promoted English business, science and enterprise.

What made Victoria dress in black?

W HEN PRINCE ALBERT DIED AT THE AGE OF 42

on December 14, 1861, Queen Victoria was devastated. She locked herself away for nearly ten years, spending time in her palaces on the Isle of Wight and at Balmoral in Scotland. She still managed to do her duties, helped by her ministers. But the British people wanted to see their queen. The prime minister, Benjamin Disraeli, convinced her to start taking on public engagements again. She obeyed but from then on she always appeared in public dressed in black as a sign of mourning for her beloved Albert.

What did people do for fun in Victorian times?

They went to the theatre, read magazines called penny dreadfuls, and played in the park. In 1851, they could also go to a grand exhibition in the Crystal Palace in London. Among the exhibits were a 24-tonne block of coal, steam engines, railway trains, a fountain that sprayed French perfume, and an early version of the typewriter. Visitors to the Crystal Palace could also admire a huge diamond called the Koh-I-Noor. Today this diamond sits on top of the queen's crown. The exhibition showed how technology was changing life in Britain for the better, with many people having more to eat and living better lives.

Who had the first Christmas tree in Britain?

Queen Victoria and Prince Albert were the first people in England to have a Christmas tree, which up until then had been a German custom. They decorated it with pears, apples, walnuts and little figures. When pictures of the royal family and their tree appeared in magazines, the fashionable members of society rushed out to buy one. A new British tradition had been established.

Crystal Palace was built for the Great Exhibition of 1851.

When was Elizabeth II born?

Her Majesty the Queen was born Elizabeth Alexandra Mary Windsor at 2.40 am on April 21, 1926 in her grandparents' house in London. She is the eldest daughter of King George VI and Queen Elizabeth, the Queen Mother. At the time of her birth, her grandfather George V was the king of England.

What was Elizabeth II like as a child?

The queen's parents were determined that she should have as normal a life as possible. In 1927, they bought a house in London for her. The address was No 145, Piccadilly and it was to be Princess Elizabeth's home until her father became king in 1936. The world was changing and the royal family knew they had to change with it. They made sure that the little princess and her sister, Princess Margaret, would not grow up spoiled or not knowing what their duties to their country were.

Queen Elizabeth II's coronation in 1953.

Where did Elizabeth II go to school?

THE QUEEN MOTHER HAD WANTED HER DAUGHTER TO be educated at a public school, but the king insisted that a future queen should not sit at the same desk as a commoner. So Princess Elizabeth had private lessons at home. She was taught by a Scottish governess called Miss Crawford, or Crawfie as the princess called her.

What did Elizabeth II do during the Second World War?

During the Second World War, the young princesses Elizabeth and Margaret stayed at Windsor Castle where they sheltered from bombing in an air-raid shelter. They also travelled to Balmoral in Scotland, and Sandringham in Norfolk. There they helped local people gather in the harvest. At the age of 18, Princess Elizabeth joined the Auxiliary Territorial Services, and by the end of the war she had become a junior commander. Both princesses joined in the celebrations marking the end of the war. As no one recognized them, they took great delight in knocking people's hats off their heads!

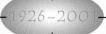

Queen Elizabeth II as she looks today.

What does Queen Elizabeth do each day?

The queen's main role is to safeguard the constitution of the country, making sure that elected governments act in the interests of the people. She and her family also promote Britain abroad. Every morning, the queen reads some of the 200 to 300 letters she receives each day. They are all answered by her staff. The queen also looks at papers sent to her by members of the government.

When did Elizabeth become queen?

PRINCESS ELIZABETH BECAME QUEEN ON FEBRUARY 6, 1952

following the death of her father George VI. She was on a Commonwealth tour in Kenya, Africa, when she heard the news. She immediately returned to London, and was met at Heathrow airport by her uncle the Duke of Gloucester and the Prime Minister Winston Churchill. The queen was then crowned in Westminster Abbey on June 2, 1953. Many people bought television sets just so that they could watch the ceremony. It made the coronation the first great television event in the history of the world.

What kind of people does Elizabeth II meet?

The queen meets a number of important people, like ambassadors from other countries, Church officials and government ministers. She also goes out on public engagements, visiting hospitals, factories and schools. At 7.30 pm each evening, she receives a report from parliament. Then she might go to a film premier, a concert or a party organized by one of her many charities. After that, she often works late into the night, looking at more government papers.

What are the queen's favourite pets?

The queen has always loved animals. Her father, George VI, started a family tradition of keeping corgis as pets and the queen is happy to keep it going.

When did Elizabeth marry?

During the war, Princess Elizabeth had fallen in love with the dashing Prince Philip of Greece, a third cousin who had lived most of his life in western Europe. Her parents were not so sure that her young romance would provide her with a suitable husband. But Queen Mary, the princess's grandmother, knew that Elizabeth was serious and she considered Prince Philip a good addition to the royal family. So Princess Elizabeth married Philip Mountbatten, Duke of Edinburgh, on November 20, 1947. Today, they have three sons, one daughter and six grandchildren.

THE FUTURE RULER?

When it comes to choosing the next ruler of Britain, the boys in the family are always chosen before the girls. That means the eldest prince in the family follows his mother or father to the throne. If there are no boys, then the girls might become queens, chosen according to age. If there are no children to inherit the throne, the brother of the king might rule in his place. At the moment, Prince Charles is heir to the crown.

Index